Gallery Books
Editor: Peter Fallon

TERESA'S BAR

By the same author

Endsville (with Brian Lynch), New Writers Press, Dublin, 1967
O Westport in the Light of Asia Minor, Anna Livia Press, Dublin,
     1975
Sam's Cross, Profile Press, Dublin, 1978
Jesus, Break His Fall, Raven Arts Press, Dublin, 1980
Ark of the North, Raven Arts Press, Dublin, 1982
The Selected Paul Durcan, Blackstaff Press, Belfast, 1982 (Poetry
     Ireland Choice), 1985
Jumping the Train Tracks with Angela, Raven Arts Press, Dublin /
     Carcanet New Press, Manchester, 1983
The Berlin Wall Café, Blackstaff Press, Belfast, 1985 (Poetry Book
     Society Choice)

Paul Durcan

TERESA'S
BAR

Gallery Books

This revised edition of
Teresa's Bar
is first published
simultaneously in paperback
and in a clothbound edition
on 10 December 1986.

The Gallery Press
19 Oakdown Road
Dublin 14, Ireland

ISBN 0 902996 49 5 (*paperback*)
0 902996 48 7 (*clothbound*)

The Gallery Press receives financial assistance from An Chomhairle
Ealaíon / The Arts Council, Ireland.

Contents

To Sarah and Síabhra

As does any other man on earth, I come from
a family and from a particular place.

Pope John XXIII

Who's gonna throw that minstrel boy a coin
Who's gonna let it roll
Who's gonna throw that minstrel boy a coin
Who's gonna let it down easy to save his soul

Bob Dylan

Sylvester Furlong's Quadrille

Sylvester Furlong is a hairdresser by profession
Who cuts his own hair when no one else is looking
In the image and likeness of his dear dead father
Who looks out from a daguerreotype, a lost leader
Marooned on an island by history's fickle seas
(Died at Passchendaele 1917);
Parting down the middle and pencil-line moustache,
Short back-and-sides but royal use of oil;
He changes white coat twice a day, not weekly,
And his gleaming shoes are patent leather black;
To all customers he is partial as a priest
And he cradles in his palms a rocker's locks
Or crew-cut carapace of a dour policeman;
The hair of half the town has reposed
At one time or another in Sylvester's bin;
And always he has a dream of his dear dead father
Dancing with his mother at the Resurrection
And they with her parents and his parents also
And Sylvester himself with an ideal wife;
But, social solitary, unmarried but unbowed,
He weaves his steel comb, a conductor's baton
Or the king of the fairies' sparkling wand;
While he leaps around the chair he quadrilles gently
And pipingly intones:
'I-am-today-what-this-man-was
And-one-day-I-shall-be-what-he-is'.

Protestant Old Folks Coach Tour
of the Ring of Kerry

Although it was a summer's day
It rained as though it was winter;
And I pressed my nose against the windowpane,
The zoo-like windowpane of the coach,
And I closed my eyes and dreamed,
Dreamed that I was swimming,
Swimming in the coves of Kerry
With my young man Danny
And no one else about;
Danny, Danny, dripping wet,
Laughing through his teeth;
Blown to bits at Ypres.
Behind my eyes it is sunshine still
Though he has gone;
And my mother and father pad about the farm
Like ghosts cut out of cardboard;
When they died I too looked ghostly
But I stayed alive though I don't know how;
Dreaming to put the beehives back on their feet,
Waiting for Danny to come home.
And now I'm keeping house for brother Giles
Who stayed at home today to milk the cows;
Myself, I am a great jowled cow untended
And when I die I would like to die alone.

The Difficulty that is Marriage

We disagree to disagree, we divide, we differ;
Yet each night as I lie in bed beside you
And you are faraway curled up in sleep
I array the moonlit ceiling with a mosaic of question-marks;
How was it I was so lucky to have ever met you?
I am no brave pagan proud of my mortality
Yet gladly on this changeling earth I should live for ever
If it were with you, my sleeping friend.
I have my troubles and I shall always have them
But I should rather live with you for ever
Than exchange my troubles for a changeless kingdom.
But I do not put you on a pedestal or throne;
You must have your faults but I do not see them.
If it were with you, I should live for ever.

The Man who Buried his Wife in the Back Garden

Each winter morning he looks out the bedroom window
At her headstone of limestone in the garden corner
Under the creosote eaves of the derelict garage,
Looks out dispassionately upon the forlorn stone
Before shuffling downstairs to make himself breakfast.
He knows that his neighbours say he's mad,
He has seen them point him out to their friends and cousins,
But he knows all too well that he is sane,
Sane as a wet blanket wrapped round a burning child.
He knows that wells of marriage have no bottoms
And that she'll not be coming back again from their well;
And the garden grass is uncut, green, and dark,
And he dreams what it would be like to wade through it
And staring at the teaspoon in the teacup
He overhears them talking to each other fifty years ago:
'Agatha, life would be unimaginable without you'
'Arthur'.

A Day in the Life of Immanuel Kant

For reasons which he least of all can comprehend
People tend to confuse Immanuel Kant
With a well-known eighteenth-century German philosopher
Of the same name; our man
Knows nothing about either Germany or philosophy
And the idea of either gives him 'a pain in the neck'
(Saying this, he never fails to rub his neck –
A thick round trunk of coarse reddened flesh)
And as for the eighteenth century – it is prehistory to him
For whom all history except for 1798
(There's a youth with pike in the town square)
Began yesterday or possibly last week
And otherwise is a filthy big cloud on the mind's horizon;
This dark horizon is rimmed by mountains of prejudice
Which serve satisfactorily to shut out sunlight
And deposit surpluses of *lebensraum* for all those things that matter
Such as motor-cars, tv, and malicious gossip spiced with pious guff:
No, he is not the Kant of Königsberg;
It happened thus: his father was off the drink
When the boy was born
And the father was adamant – 'adamant' he said –
That his son should be christened Immanuel;
The mother protested but her adamant husband told her to . . . .
The boy grew up to be a manly Christian lad,
A powerful hurler and petrified of women,
And became like his father, an auctioneer,
A respectable member of the criminal classes,
A zealous anti-Semite and a decent Catholic,
And now in middle-age he is enjoying the fruits of his labours.

His 'little wifey' brings him up breakfast in bed each morning
After which he herds the brood to school
In the de luxe saloon. Then he works for an hour
Before going home to play with his toys until dinner-time –

Drilling holes in walls like an assassin berserk with a gun.
In the afternoon, after one more hour of work,
He takes a constitutional by the river, stopping
To spit every now and then,
Home then to Wifey, the Box and the Six-Pack,
The two brats and the possibility of copulation.
We will begin today's lecture with the problem of copulation
But first of all we must cut down that tree in the back garden.

Lord Mayo

I had to go and work in office-blocks in Shepherd's Bush
   And I worked such hours that I could not write letters;
I spent my few hours in The Railway Tavern talking
   With a Carlow-born clerk and two Belfast bricklayers;
But I came back to you, Lord Mayo.

Now you are older and angrier and I am still young and gay
   And what, my lord, are we going to do?
If you were but to smile once as once you used to
   I'd jump into bed with you for ever;
For I came back to you, Lord Mayo.

I'd go live with you in the wilds of Erris
   Rearing children despite bog and rain;
I'd row with you the dark depths of Beltra and of Conn
   If you'd but smile on me;
For I came back to you, Lord Mayo.

The Seminary

High up above the town on a spur of rock
Towers the seminary
Which once was our small town's dormant volcano
And source of trade
But now the seminarians are detaching themselves from it like lava
And our fathers and mothers are strewn about the streets and terraces
Prostrate in their perplexity;
Nor have we got, nor do we expect to get,
Help from the Italian pope;
I say like lava but sometimes like fire itself;
Last week our most distinguished seminarian,
A student of the classics and a most courteous creature,
When he heard that his mother had been written to by the rector
About her son's ecumenical views
And that it had been arranged for her to pay her son a visit,
The gangling boy climbed up the fire-escape to the top-most roof-top
Sheer above the river far below
And launching himself off into space
Broke himself into smithereens upon the waters' back.
Now peering down into his wat'ry grave
I think of what his young life might have been
If only pride of humility had obtained;
If Angelo Roncalli had paid a visit to this town
Rectors and bishops would have had to hightail it
And perhaps, God willing, they'd have never come back;
'As does any other man on earth,
I come from a family and from a particular place';
But Roncalli is no more paid heed to
Than Gregory the Great
And the reign of Pius XII has been resumed –
He of the telephone and the solitary table
And the electric razor and the single-seater gold-plated cadillac;
Like some vast museum of a declining empire
The seminary is falling down.

The Hat Factory

Eleven o'clock and the bar is empty
Except for myself and an old man;
We sit with our backs to the street-window,
The sun in the east streaming through it;
And I think of childhood and swimming
Underwater by a famine pier;
The ashlar coursing of the stonework
Like the bar-room shelves
Seen through tidal amber seaweed
In the antique mirror;
Now myself and the old man floating
In the glow of the early morning sun
Twined round each other and our newspapers;
And our pintglasses like capstans on the pier.
We do not read our daily charters
– Charters of liberty to know what's going on –
But hold them as capes before reality's bull
And with grace of ease we make our passes;
El Cordobes might envy this old small man
For the sweet veronicas he makes in daily life.
He is the recipient of an old age pension
While such is my niche in society's scale
I do not rate even the dole
But I am at peace with myself and so is he;
Although I do not know what he is thinking
His small round fragile noble mouth
Has the look of the door of Aladdin's cave
Quivering in expectation of the magic word;
Open sesame;
I suspect that like me he is thinking
Of the nothing-in-particular;
Myself, I am thinking of the local hat factory,
Of its history and the eerie fact
That in my small town I have never known

Anyone who worked in it
Or had to do with it at all;
As a child I used look through a hole in the hedge
At the hat factory down below in the valley;
I used lie flat on my face in the long grass
And put out my head through the hole;
Had the hatters looked out through their porthole windows
They would have seen high up in the hillside
A long wild hedgerow broken only
By the head of the child looking out through the hole;
I speculate;
And as to what kind of hats they make;
And do they have a range in black birettas;
And do they have a conveyor belt of toppers;
And do the workers get free hats?
And I recall the pope's skull-cap
Placed on my head when as a boy-child
In a city hospital I lay near to death
And the black homburg of the red-nosed undertaker
And the balaclavas of assassins
And the pixies of the lost children of the murdered earth;
And the multi-coloured yamulka of the wandering Jew
And the black kippa of my American friend
In Jerusalem in the snow
And the portly Egyptian's tiny fez
And the tragic Bedouin's kefia in the sands of sun
And the monk's cowl and the nun's wimple
And the funereal mortarboards of airborn puritans
And the megalithic coifs of the pan-cake women of Brittany
And the sleek fedoras of well-to-do thugs
And sadistic squires' napoleonic tricorns
And prancing horse-cavalry in their cruel shakos
And the heroic lifeboatman's black sou'wester
And the nicotine-stained wig of the curly-haired barrister

And the black busby used as a handbag by my laughing brother
And the silken turban of the highbrow widow
And foreign legionaries in nullah kepis
And mayday praesidiums in astrakhans
And bonnets and boaters and sombreros and stetsons
And stove-pipes and steeples and mantillas and berets
And topis and sun-hats and deer-stalkers and pill-boxes
And naughty grandmothers in toques
And bishops' mitres and soldiers' helmets;
And in Languedoc and in Aran – cloth caps.
And what if you were a hatter
And you married a hatter
And all your sons and daughters worked as hatters
And you inhabited a hat-house all full of hats:
Hats, hats, hats, hats:
Hats: the apotheosis of an ancient craft
And I think of all the nationalities of Israel
And of how each always clings to his native hat,
His priceless and moveable roof,
His hat which is the last and first symbol
Of a man's slender foothold on this earth.
Women and girls also work in the factory
But not many of them wear hats;
Some wear scarves, but rarely hats;
Now there'll be no more courting of maidens
In schooner hats on dangerous cliffs;
It seems part of the slavery of liberation
To empty relationships of all courtship
Of which hats were an exciting part.
Probably, I shall never wear a hat:
So thus I ask the old man
If I may look at his trilby
– Old honesty –
And graciously he hands it to me

And with surprise
I note that it was manufactured
In the local hat factory
And I hand it back to him
– A crown to its king –
And like a king he blesses me when he goes
Wishing me a good day before he starts
His frail progress home along the streets,
Along the lanes and terraces of the hillside,
To his one up and one down.
I turn about and see
Over the windowpane's frosted hemisphere
A small black hat sail slowly past my eyes
Into the unknown ocean of the sun at noon.

Wife Who Smashed Television Gets Jail

'She came home, my Lord, and smashed-in the television;
Me and the kids were peaceably watching Kojak
When she marched into the living-room and declared
That if I didn't turn off the television immediately
She'd put her boot through the screen;
I didn't turn it off, so instead she turned it off
– I remember the moment exactly because Kojak
After shooting a dame with the same name as my wife
Snarled at the corpse – Goodnight, Queen Maeve –
And then she took off her boots and smashed-in the television;
I had to bring the kids round to my mother's place;
We got there just before the finish of Kojak;
(My mother has a fondness for Kojak, my Lord);
When I returned home my wife had deposited
What was left of the television into the dustbin,
Saying – I didn't get married to a television
And I don't see why my kids or anybody else's kids
Should have a television for a father or mother,
We'd be much better off all down in the pub talking
Or playing bar-billiards –
Whereupon she disappeared off back down again to the pub.'
Justice O'Brádaigh said wives who preferred bar-billiards to
      family television
Were a threat to the family which was the basic unit of society
As indeed the television itself could be said to be the basic unit of
      the family
And when as in this case wives expressed their preference in
      forms of violence
Jail was the only place for them. Leave to appeal was refused.

Polycarp

Polycarp has quit the priesthood
And he is living back at home;
He wears a smile upon his lips
That blooms from the marrow bone.

It's a smile that flowers and withers
Like fruit upon a tree;
In winter he stands at corners
In the streets all nakedly.

They are waxing pretty angry –
Are Respectability's crew;
It's a crime against all decency
To be one of the very few

Who has had courage like Polycarp
To be his own sweet self;
Not to mind the small town sneers
When they call him a 'fucking elf'

Or the do-it-yourself-men boors
Who detest men with feminine souls;
Boors who when they were boys
Spoke of women as 'ruddy holes'

And now who are married and proper
Living up on Respectability Hill
And in their spare time make their own coffins
Which they use first as coffee tables.

But Polycarp polkas the streets
As free and easy as he feels;
Sometimes he walks on his toes,
Sometimes on his heels.

Yet they'll put him upon his knees
In the amphitheatre soon;
But his smile will wear them down
By the blood-light of the moon;

And in summer's golden rains
He'll burst out in fruit all over;
She's here, she's here, she's here;
And it is Polycarp that knows how to love her.

Swags of red apples are his cheeks;
Swags of yellow pears are his eyes;
Foliages of dark green oaks are his torsos;
And in the cambium of his bark juice lies.

Desire under the steeples and spires,
Polycarp's back in town;
Desire under the steeples and spires,
Polycarp's back in town.

Alice's Palace beside the Cemetery

To think that one day you will be a heap of bones
In the cemetery behind the back garden wall
And yet here you are at home on a winter's afternoon
Standing up naked in front of your looking-glass.
Spire of mortuary chapel behind your left shoulder
And cross-word puzzle of crosses under your arm,
Combing out the long mane of your river-brown hair,
A hair-pin between your pink lips;
Some think you ought use
Your few score of years
Down on your knees repeating your prayers
But not you: not for you the fastidious fevers
Of daughters who will not make love in the same house as
    their mothers
Or of the living who will not live next door to the dead;
You comb your hair forward until it falls down your face
Like a waterfall down the door of a cave;
Until you throw back your head, and you toss back your hair
Splashing your fingers through it;
And you step back with your hands on your hips,
Painted fingernails splayed on your hipbones;
Your cheekbones etched on the looking-glass;
And you whisper to your lover in your bed
To move over –
It's a dark cold day, alive, alive O –

The Drover's Path Murder

The drover's path slopes round between the bog-edge
And the mountainside and along it on a winter's night
The beautifullest woman in West Mayo walked home.
But she was known not merely for her ebony curls
And her billowing bosom on which no man had slept
And her narrow waist and legs that blossomed into thighs –
Trees with their heads in the clouds;
She was known also for her jewellery, all pure gold,
Which she carried about with her, wherever she went.
So, on a winter's night two men lay in wait for her
Behind a moon-lit boulder on the drover's path;
Fiercely she fought them but they pinned her down
And searched her savagely but could find no gold.
They raped and murdered her because they could find no gold;
She had hidden it, as had long been her practice,
On winter's night journeys along the drover's path,
In the roots of her curls, long fabled in Mayo,
And over the tangled roots she had knotted her hair
Until all under a black mass the yellow gold lay concealed.

Now in a gale-attacked sun-lit February day
Years later, as with men I work at men's trades,
Fencing off mountains to fence in sheep,
And our hands too numb to grasp pliers and hacksaw,
And our lives in danger from the bog concealed in water,
Five miles to be walked over before dry land is reached,
We look over and upward at the drover's path,
Where the beautifullest woman in West Mayo was murdered;
That it is a black spot is demonstrably evident
For it gives off of itself a malodorous shadow
From which even the sheep and the goats steer clear.
As three men, thrice murderous, we bow our heads,
Yet soon we too may have to pay with our lives
And we shall have only our faces for gold,
Only our faces for gold.

I stare at the murder-spot and recall many faces
Of dead sheep floating upwards in the glittering bog
And will I ever see them again, not to speak of myself,
In the mirror of a day that would know not one murder
But only the warmth of women and of women's voices?

Anna Swanton

I met her on the road to Ballavarry;
She asked me why do boys always hurry;
And when I told her I had the train to take
She turned and said she'd come and wave goodbye.

Along that wide road blue green and dusty
That lopes along the land to Ballavarry
I listened to her words come over to me
As from over the most deserted ancient valley.

We walked along the platform at Ballavarry;
I stopped to pluck daisies to make a chain;
I put it round her neck and though it parted
I did not make another for we have not.

For the train no more stopped at Ballavarry;
It had stopped for the last time the week before;
Next year we got the stationmaster's cottage
And our children are growing up playing real trains.

And yet although I live in terror of the tracks
For fear that they should prove our children's grave
I live in greater terror of the thought
Of life without Anna Swanton on this earth;

Or of how I might be rich in far-off Nottingham
And married to another kind of girl;
I'd rather rain for ever in the fields with Anna Swanton
Than a car or a goddess in the sun.

Three Hundred Men Made Redundant

It is shocking, Hilda, shocking;
300 men made redundant;
I have to collect a sirloin at the butcher's;
I'll see you at the hairdresser's in half-an-hour.

300 men made redundant;
Indeed, indeed, how shocking, how shocking;
I forgot to tell Madge about the card-game for Sunday;
If I see her at the hairdresser's I'll tell her then.

Good day, Fr Ryan, I'm very well, how are you?
Thanks be to God and His Holy Mother;
300 men made redundant;
Perfectly shocking, perfectly shocking.

Kindly, Fr Ryan, give the pulpit a clean-up;
I find the handrail has become a bit sticky;
Which reminds me I must make a note of it;
300 men made redundant.

But we have bigger issues to thrash out
Than 300 men made redundant;
For example the evils of family planning –
Not to mention mixed marriages and mixed education.

(*Sing*) 300 men made redundant
       300 men made redundant
       300 men made redundant
       – And the evils of family planning.

Percy and Jane

They live in a house by the sea
Not a bit like you or like me;
Though they practise monogamy
They call it polygamy
And they're as happy as ever can be.

She Mends an Ancient Wireless

You never claimed to be someone special;
Sometimes you said you had no special talent;
Yet I have seen you rear two dancing daughters
With care and patience and love unstinted;
Reading or telling stories, knitting gansies
And all the while holding down a job
In the teeming city, morning until dusk.
And in the house when anything went wrong
You were the one who fixed it without fuss;
The electricity switch which was neither on nor off,
The tv aerial forever falling out;
And now as I watch you mend an ancient wireless
From my tiny perch I cry once more your praises
And call out your name aross the great divide – Nessa.

Mabel

Mabel, all you ever want to do is to make love;
You never simply want to prance or walk;
You never want to hear my effusive talk
Concerning marriage and life above
For man and woman in the marriage tub;
You never want the man not to touch her;
You never want to devour with me a butcher;
You never want to imbibe with me a pub;
You never want to inaugurate with me a boutique;
You never want to pray with me in Arabic;
You never want to read with me the Koran;
You never dream of life with me above;
All you ever want to do is to make love;
What do you think I am? A man?

Trauma Junction

The answer to your question is that I am not your mother;
Your mother was another mother and she died in Russia.

Him

His name was Christmas and he was a refugee;
And he moved through his exile like waves through a landless sea.

Bugs Bunny

There is a schoolteacher in my town and he looks like Bugs Bunny:
He is a mass murderer and I am not being funny.

Cahirciveen Labour Exchange

We all do not live in a yellow submarine –
Scream the unemployed of Cahirciveen.

Teresa's Bar

We sat all day in Teresa's Bar
And talked, or did not talk, the time away;
The only danger was that we might not leave sober
But that is a price you have to pay.
Outside in the rain the powers-that-be,
Chemist, draper, garda, and priest
Paced up and down in unspeakable rage
That we could sit all day in Teresa's Bar
'Doing nothing'.

Behind the bar it was often empty;
Teresa, like all of us,
Besides doing nothing
Had other things to do
Such as cooking meals
Or washing out underwear
For her mad father
And her madder husband
Or enduring their screams.

But Teresa deep down had no time for time
Or for those whose business has to do with time;
She would lean against the bar and smile through her weariness
By turns being serious and light with us;
Her eyes were birds on the waves of the sea;
A mother-figure but also a sun-girl;
An image of tranquility but of perpetual creation;
A process in which there is no contradiction
For those with guts not to be blackmailed by time.

There is no time in Teresa's Bar;
The Garda Síochána or the Guardia Civil –
The Junior Chamber or the Roman Curia –
The Poetry Society or the G.A.A. –

The Rugby Club or the Maynooth Hierarchy –
R.T.E. or Conor's Cabaret –
It makes no difference in Teresa's Bar
Where the air is as annotated with the tobacco smoke of inventiveness
As the mind of a Berkeleyan philosopher.

The small town abounds with rumours
About Teresa's Bar;
A hive of drug-takers (poor bees)
A nest of fornicators (poor birds)
Homosexual not to mention heterosexual;
Poor birds and bees trapped in metaphors of malice.
The truth is that here as along by the path
By the river that flows along by the edge of the town
Young and old meet in a life-obtaining sequence
Of days interspersed by nights, seasons by seasons,
Deaths by deaths;
While the members of the society of judgement
Growl and scowl behind arrases in drawing-rooms
Here are the members of the resurrection of life
And their tutelary goddess is Teresa.
Thirty-five, small, heavy, and dark,
And who would sleep with any man who was honest enough
Not to mouth the platitudes of love;
A sensual woman, brave and true,
Bringer of dry wisdom and free laughter
As well as of glasses and bowls,
And who has sent forth into the hostile world
Persons whose universal compassion is infinitesimally more catholic
Than that of any scion of académe
Such as James Felix Hennessey
Who has been on the dole for sixteen years
As well as making poems and reading books
And who when accused of obscenity

By the Right Rev. Fr O'Doherty
Riposted with all the humility of Melchisedech:
'You must learn the reality of the flesh, Father;
You must learn the reality of the flesh'.

If there be a heaven
Heaven would be
Being with Teresa
Inside the rain;
So let's lock up the bar Teresa,
Lay ourselves on the floor,
Put some more coal on the fire,
Pour ourselves each a large whiskey;
Let's drink to Teresa of Teresa's Bar
Reclining on the floor with one of her boys,
And big black coals burning bright,
And yellowest whiskey in a brown bottle,
And outside a downpour relentlessly pouring down.

The Baker

After a night at the ovens
In the big city bakery
The baker walks home alone:
He stalks through the dawn
Gropingly
Like a man through a plate-glass door
(There have been many such –
Oh many such – years
And nights of it
And it has been so
Hot)
He feels fragile and eerily pure
Like a loaf new out of oven,
All heat through-and-through,
And he does not look sure
That the air is not a plate-glass door;
Gropingly he stalks
In his hob-nailed boots
Up the steep terraced street:
A tiny giant walking in glue:
A human being about to split in two.

Two in a Boat

She took one oar and I took the other
But mine had slipped from me when she pulled on hers;
And then when at last I had got a grip
She had raised hers in victory glittering over sable waters,
The sun merely accentuating victory's glitter in each pearly
    globule.
And so we pulled in opposite directions,
Drifting out of quarrels into accidents and out of accidents into
    quarrels.
I thought of our two children in another country and of their
    being free
From their parents until came a collision
With two other frail craft and later
Drifting onto a grass bank we had to be pushed out into the sun
    again.
But the sun did not alter the pattern until out of the blue
Came glorious fresh rain
And pulling in opposite directions we reached land again.

Deserted in Doolin

neither sea-currach nor mini-car bid welcome

on me the gods have turned their backs
whose sykes-shadows are on cliffs and in skies

I cry a Crab Island Blues but to no avail
I am deserted in Doolin – please hear me

oh follow me down to Doolin, Dan,
but only on a summer's morn.

The Weeping Headstones of the Isaac Becketts

The Protestant graveyard was a forbidden place
So naturally as children we explored its precincts:
Clambered over drystone walls under elms and chestnuts,
Parted long grasses and weeds, poked about under yews,
Reconnoitred the chapel whose oak doors were always closed,
Stared at the schist headstones of the Isaac Becketts.
Then we would depart with mortal sins in our bones
As ineradicable as an arthritis;
But we had seen enough to know what the old folks meant
When we would overhear them whisperingly at night refer to
'The headstones of the Becketts – they would make you weep'.
These arthritises of sin:
But although we had only six years each on our backs
We could decipher
Brand-new roads open up through heaven's fields
And upon them – like thousands upon thousands
Of people kneeling in the desert –
The weeping headstones of the Isaac Becketts.

In Memory of Those Murdered in the Dublin Massacre, May 1974

In the grime-ridden sunlight in the downtown Wimpy bar
I think of all the crucial aeons – and of the labels
That freedom fighters stick onto the lost destinies of unborn children
The early morning sunlight carries in the whole street from outside;
The whole wide street from outside through the plate-glass windows
Wholly, sparklingly, surgingly, carried in from outside;
And the waitresses cannot help but be happy and gay
As they swipe at the table-tops with their dishcloths –
Such a moment as would provide the heroic freedom fighter
With his perfect meat.
And I think of those heroes – heroes? – and how truly
Obscene is war.

And as I stand up to walk out –
The aproned old woman who's been sweeping the floor
Has mop stuck in bucket, leaning on it;
And she's trembling all over, like a flower in the breeze.
She'd make a mighty fine explosion now, if you were to blow her up
An explosion of petals, of aeons, and the waitresses too, flying
      breasts and limbs,
For a free Ireland.

June 1974

And so we are in Mountrath and not, as we thought, in the
Khyber Pass.
At the far end of the street high up in the blank window of a
police barracks
I can see the telescopic lens of a rifle glint in the June
afternoon sunlight
But I do not mind, I am talking to the friend of a friend,
A fellow-olympian in the matchstick mountains, for whom the
only arms
Are the arms of a woman beloved. Behind the rifle pointed at
me
God knows who may be crouching – Churchmen in His name
Now are stalking the land's borders with bombs under their skirts
Plus wads of boat-money for unmarried mothers of boys
Who after swift, ungolden, Clapham childhoods
Of loneliness, poverty, and religion,
Will come home to die for the old sod and the Khyber Pass and
Ireland.
Friend, be past minding. I sing with you
All women and children and old men and old women today in the
sun in Mountrath.

Maud Gonne MacBride's Mayo

Over at where the stream went under the ground
Under the orchard wall
A dog, a black and white terrier, yelped at the vanishing water.

I saw the chaperones and the girls
As though they had been born but should never die;
The chaperones who had turned away
From the cool white core of the wood
To lean on tip-toe on the cliff-edge of the meadow;
And at the cool white core
Under the low strung streaming branches of the oak
Sleeping girls lay floating on their backs
Above the winding grass;
Increase of light did not shut their eyes
Nor the old horse that later staggered past
As though by accident;
Past the well full of floating leaves
And the teacups that were filling with clay.

And the big house loomed as though either empty or not.

The clouds – doves from Africa – marked time in the hill:
Then it came:
In spite of their nakedness – such sea floor and such waves –
The sleeping girls burst into rain
As though they were the fire inside the rain;
And their faces were flashed onto the windowpanes
Of all trains leaving Paris for the East
And they went out over the same stile,
        The same fall,
Like raindrops off the peak of a boy king's cap.

In some twigs stood a vast cathedral roofless,
Its forests of red spires yearning for her milky breast.

Before the Celtic Yoke

What was it like in Ireland before the Celtic yoke –
Before war insinuated its slime into the forests of the folk?

Elizabethan, Norman, Viking, Celt,
Conquistadores all:
Imperialists, racialists, from across the seas,
Merciless whalesback riders
Thrusting their languages down my virgin throat,
And to rape not merely but to garotte
My human voice:
To screw my soul to orthodoxy and break my neck.

But I survive, recall
That these are but Micky-come-latelies
Puritanical, totalitarian, by contrast with my primal tongue:
My vocabularies are boulders cast up on time's beaches;
Masses of sea-rolled stones reared up in mile-high ricks
Along the shores and curving coasts of all my island;
Verbs dripping fresh from geologic epochs;
Scorched, drenched, in metamorphosis, vulcanicity, ice ages.

No Celt
Nor Viking, Norman, Elizabethan,
Could exterminate me –
I am as palpable and inscrutable
As is a mother to her man-child;
If you would contemplate me
You will know the terror that an old man knows
As he shrinks back from the grassy womb of his chirping mamma.

In Ireland before the Celtic yoke I was the voice of Seeing
And my island people's Speaking was their Being;
So go now brother – cast off all cultural shrouds
And speak like me – like the mighty sun through the clouds.

Goodbye Tipperary

In a small town under Tipperary hills
She thought she was in Czechoslovakia,
House-fronts painted but not at the rears.
We had been through a long day's work up in high cold fields
And we had not met before and time was scarce;
The bar roof over our heads was low
And you could see night congregating outside the door.
She had been born during the war in Massachusetts
Of a Scots Protestant father and an English Catholic mother –
From birth a creature of religion's wars and exile.
But being a serious woman, she laughed, she laughed much.
We spoke each at the same time, listening hard,
So that while I was telling her about our Irish tolerance
Of everything except women and freedom of conscience,
She was saying how inside her head she could hear
The tramp-a-tramp tramp-a-tramp tramp tramp tramp
Of a Soviet paratrooper overheard on the railway carriage
As her train crossed over the border from Vienna into Bratislava.
She was not a gambler or a drinker, she said, although once
She had put a bet for her father on a horse called Wessex Gold;
'My mother said he was drunk but I paid no heed –
That was when I was young and wise.' And again
She gritted her eyes so deeply bright that even yet to recall her
I can see under a mountain stream's black waters
The yellow sands staying.
Then in the dark a whistle blew and
Doors banged, and voices shrieked, and
Goodbyes got somehow wrung.
Goodbye Tipperary.

Where Three Fields Meet

But when she sang: And after Spring
Can Winter be far behind?
Her father appealed to the bone-eyed piper,
May we take it from the start again?

For when she was three and a child of the sun
Long before her father, long before he
Came down from the skies like rain,
An old man laughed, Where is the Summer?

And: It is out at the sea, cried she.
It is out at the sea, laughed they.
And it rained it rained it rained
A spear green through.

The Crown of Widowhood

When the black and yellow motor-car sprang around the
    street-corner
– Black roof, yellow body –
And drove over her straight between the shoulderblades
She was walking up the main street deep in thought
Wearing the crown of widowhood.

Though it was a winter's day her face was sunlight
And her eyes were freshwaters alive with trout leaping
And she was a delicate creature in flight treading stepping-stones;
She was a walking, talking, Japanese gardens
Wearing the crown of widowhood.

But though it was a winter's day the driver wore sunglasses
And a tiny black hat perched in his white fuzzy hair
And a tiny white cigarette in his red, blue, face;
He did not see her, and he would never see her
Wearing the crown of widowhood.

He was transporting a rocking-chair on the motor-car roof-rack
Which he had bought cheap at a small auction
And he was bringing it back home to show to himself;
He was God and he had no time for man or woman
Wearing the crown of widowhood.

The Friary Golf Club

They do not like me at the local golf club
But take my green fee out of some necessity.
The green keeper is secretary because in early days
He seduced a daughter of the local gentry
And they in holy matrimony were joined
And she now tends the bar.
Faithful sheep such as the parish priest
Bleat in all climes for her
While her massive husband – she being a
   creature minuscule in all –
Revolves about the golf course in a farmyard tractor
Glowering at players as they seek to hit
Past monastic ruins on the seventh fairway.
Did monks who prayed here in the fourteenth century
Envisage tiny white discs in flight through the air
Being chased by human beings with clubs and sticks?
Can you, golfer, at your twentieth century ritual
Envisage monks at prayer here in the fourteenth century?
For where now your golf ball reclines astutely
A prior sunbathed in the grass;
But the parish priest in the golf club bar intones:
'Thou shalt not imagine anything'.

The Archbishop Dreams of the Harlot of Rathkeale

My dream is non-committal – it is no sin –
(Thomas, I think, would be tickled by it –
As indeed I am myself; in it is a neat point).
I am simply lying here in my double-bed
Dreaming of the harlot of Rathkeale;
I see her walking down the road at evening
Wearing a red scarf and black high-heel shoes;
She is wearing nothing else and the sun
In the western sky is a-dying slowly
In a blue sky half as old as time;
A car approaches her but from behind
Resembling palely an approaching elephant
Seen through binoculars in the bush;
It does not halt – I think the driver
Is too shocked – he looks back aghast –
A god-fearing man – and in my dream, I laugh
And say her name out aloud in my mind
'Esmé – Esmé, the harlot of Rathkeale';
She is walking towards me when the dream ends
And I wake up in the morning feeling like an old bull
Plumb to charge through my brethren in my sermon.

Mr Newspapers

The small town lies at the end of a long valley,
A disc of light at the end of a long dark tunnel.
On one side of the valley on a peak of a ridge
Crouches a huge gothic red-brick pile
With dormer windows and campanile;
It used to be known as the county home
But now it is known as the psychiatric hospital.
Dr Ryan – Dr Alphonsus Ryan – operates a personal gulag
'Specialising' as he opines 'in drop-outs' –
A rabbit-dropping phrase
Which drops out of his visor-visaged tight-lipped mouth
Not less than thirty-five times a day;
He opines that there should be a law whereby
'Drop-outs should be compelled to work
For a two-year period of preventive detention
To get them back into a healthy way of living'.
Dr Ryan himself exemplifies the 'healthy way of living'
In a mock-Tudor detached house called 'Clonmacnoise'
Replete with mahogany sideboards of silverware
And bookshelves displaying the works of Len Deighton
    and Teresa of Avila.
He rides with the local hunt
And his children board at the most expensive
Fee-paying schools in Ireland.
His wife is chief witch
At coffee covens of the select elect.
Young drop-outs get special treatment from Dr Ryan;
Blitzkriegs of electric shock, and threats of leucotomy;
But the older men are not duped by Dr Ryan,
Old Mr Newspapers least of all,
Who twice weekly takes a taxi into the nearest city
And earns himself fifty pounds as a pavement artist;
He brings back cigarettes and sweets for all the boys
And they in turn keep him supplied in newspapers;

On summer's evenings he sits out on the grim veranda
Hands crossed across his chest, hat cocked back on head,
And slow-talking as the daytime stars rolling across the sky,
And as majestic,
And the well-stuffed newspapers showing from beneath
    the turn-ups of his trousers;
Would you like a Bull's Eye, he roars, a Bull's Eye?

The Kilfenora Teaboy

I'm the Kilfenora teaboy
And I'm not so very young,
But though the land is going to pieces
I will not take up the gun;
I am happy making tea,
I make lots of it when I can,
And when I can't – I just make do;
And I do a small bit of sheepfarming on the side.

It's the small bit of furze between two towns
Is what makes the Kilfenora teaboy really run.

I have nine healthy daughters
And please God I will have more,
Sometimes my dear wife beats me
But on the whole she's a gentle soul;
When I'm not making her some tea
I sit out and watch them all
Ring-a-rosying in the street;
And I do a small bit of sheepfarming on the side.

It's the small bit of furze between two towns
Is what makes the Kilfenora teaboy really run.

Oh indeed my wife is handsome,
She has a fire lighting in each eye,
You can pluck laughter from her elbows
And from her knees pour money's tears;
I make all my tea for her,
I'm her teaboy on the hill,
And I also thatch her roof;
And I do a small bit of sheepfarming on the side.

It's the small bit of furze between two towns
Is what makes the Kilfenora teaboy really run.

And I'm not only a famous teaboy,
I'm a famous caveman too;
I paint pictures by the hundred
But you can't sell walls;
Although the people praise my pictures
As well as my turf-perfumèd blend
They rarely fling a fiver in my face;
Don't we do an awful lot of dying on the side.

It's the small bit of furze between two towns
Is what makes the Kilfenora teaboy really run.

What is a Protestant, Daddy?

Gaiters were sinister
And you dared not
Glance up at the visage;
It was a long lean visage
With a crooked nose
And beaked dry lips
And streaky grey hair
And they used scurry about
In small black cars
(Unlike Catholic bishops
Stately in big cars
Or Pope Pius XII
In his gold-plated cadillac)
And they'd make dashes for it
Across deserted streets
And disappear quickly
Into vast cathedrals
All silent and aloof,
Forlorn and leafless,
Their belfry louvres
Like dead men's lips,
And whose congregations, if any,
Were all octogenarian
With names like Iris;
More likely
There were no congregations
And these rodent-like clergymen
Were conspirators;
You could see it in their faces;
But as to what the conspiracies
Were about, as children
We were at a loss to know;
Our parents called them 'parsons'
Which turned them from being rodents

Into black hooded crows
Evilly flapping their wings
About our virginal souls;
And these 'parsons' had wives –
As unimaginable a state of affairs
As it would have been to imagine
A pope in a urinal;
Protestants were Martians
Light-years more weird
Than zoological creatures;
But soon they would all go away
For as a species they were dying out.
Soon there would be no more Protestants . . .
O Yea, O Lord,
I was a proper little Irish Catholic boy
Way back in the 1950s.